AUSTRALIAN **ZEN**

A taste of Australian Zen for the seeker and curious alike, here is a book of sayings, yarns, quotes and explanations. From both past and present, the maverick spirit of Australia points to a different way of looking at the world: openly, directly, fatalistically.

In this book, Robert Treborlang elucidates the curious philosophy that emerged in the furthest corner of the world. Readers can either enjoy the true Zen of the South from the sidelines or try to apply the lessons them-selves. Either way this whimsical book will provide a feast of interest and amusement.

BOOKS BY THE SAME AUTHOR

Only in Australia

How to Be Normal in Australia

How to Survive Australia

Sydney: Discover the City

How to Make It Big in Australia

She Vomits Like a Lady

Staying Sane in Australia

Men, Women and Other Necessities

How to Mate in Australia

A Hop Through Australia's History

The Little Book of Aussie Insults

The Little Book of Aussie Wisdom

The Little Book of Aussie Manners

AUSTRALIAN ZEN

ROBERT TREBORLANG

Major Mitchell Press

To Moi Moi, beautifully Zen

All rights reserved.
No portion of this book may be reproduced –
mechanically, electronically, or by any other means, including
photocopying – without permission of the publisher.

Published 1999

Major Mitchell Press Pty Ltd
PO Box 997, Potts Point NSW 1335
Copyright © Robert Treborlang
Illustrations by Mark Knight

Design by András Berkes
Cover design by The Communique Group
Typeset by Verand Press, Sydney
Printed by McPherson's Printing Group
Clipart by New Horizons™ Educational Computing Services

National Library of Australia Cataloguing-in-Publication entry:
Treborlang, Robert:
Australian zen.
ISBN 1 875614 17 6
1. National characteristics, Australian.
2. Australia – Social life and customs.
I. Title.

AUSTRALIAN
ZEN

INTRODUCTION

Things might not be what they seem
but in Australia they are.

ROBERT TREBORLANG

I AM A FATALIST
and believe
that what will be, will be;
what is, is;
and what was, was;
and so on through the verbs.

LENNIE LOWER

SHE'LL BE RIGHT
Zen Contemplation

Perhaps no aspect of Australian Zen is as puzzling and yet intriguing to outsiders as *She'll be right*. Or as misunderstood. *She'll be right* is not a saying, nor is it a proverb designed to teach a lesson. Instead it is an integral part of a system honed over two centuries to help bring the inhabitant of the continent to a direct realization of the ultimate situation here.

Taken from the language of the sea, she ('ship') and be right ('stay afloat'), the words can be a statement, a reassurance, an exclamation, an opinion, an affirmation of faith, an expression of jest, or any other fragment of Australian Zen thinking. Currently, there are some eighteen million traditional *She'll be right* in existence.

Encountering *She'll be right* can occur on arrival at the airport when the taxi driver flings into the boot of his cab all the valuables marked 'fragile', or when he helps deliver your baby on a lonely stretch of country

road a short time later. It may literally take years of living with *She'll be right* before a visitor really understands it. But afterwards, the next generation – and they may be using it from as young an age as seven – the mysterious meaning of *She'll be right* will become embedded at the cellular level.

The great Australian Zen expert John Ironbark wrote, "If you take the words *She'll be right* and say them unceasingly, your European obsession with excellence will die and your Germanic perfectionism will be destroyed. Suddenly, it is as though a vast, magnificent golf course stretched before you, with no place to set your leaden boots. You want to play but you are wearing a space suit. Then all at once you are saying *She'll be right*, and boots and space suit are cast off as you come to experience Australian Zen in its purest form."

I GAINED NOTHING

at all from Australian Zen,
and for that very reason it is
called Australian Zen.

GAUTAMA

ONE MAN

is just as good as another,
in fact better.

HARRY HOOTON

LIFE

is mostly froth and bubble
Two things stand like stone:
Kindness in another's trouble,
Courage in your own.

ADAM LINDSAY GORDON

A
gum tree
is very Zen.

A
gum leaf
is perfect Zen.

THE MAN

that holds his own is good enough.

BANJO PATTERSON

WATCHING CRICKET
Zen Meditation 1

Traditionally, one sits on a seat or a lounge chair. The legs are stretched out, with the right foot on the left foot, or the left foot on the right ankle. The spine leans backwards slightly, letting the belly hang naturally while the shoulders are pushed back for solid support – if you lean forward, you're not practicing Australian Zen.

The head is straight, chin hangs, eyes are slightly open and cast down. Hands are placed in the lap and wrapt around something – left hand usually around a snack, the right around a tin or a bottle – lightly touching as to form an oval.

The position must be kept with great care.

In the words of cricketing monk Henry Everingham:

"When we sit like this, even though our team might be ten thousand k's away, we have become as one. The position requires total immobility. You can't afford to let your concentration wane for even one instance.

17

This is the most important lesson: You can sit there and watch two men in partnership for two hours and then lose your concentration with disastrous results. It happened to me many times on the way to Australian Cricket Zenhood: I made a cup of tea and Australia collapsed."

It's a Zen thing – we are there for them. All is one in the universe. But you may find that when the most dedicated cricketing monk breaks that Zen consciousness to take a leak, he places not just himself, or the cricket team, but entire Australia in danger.

I'D RATHER WALK
down Hunter street
And meet a man I like to meet,
And talk with him about old times,
And how the market is for rhymes
Between two drinks, than hold commune
Upon a mountain with the moon.

VICTOR DALEY

THE TINY,

not the immense,
Will teach our groping eyes.

FRANCIS WEBB

BREAD

is a large number of small holes
entirely surrounded by bread.

LENNIE LOWER

THE AVERAGE
IS DIVINE.

KEITH HANCOCK

DRIVE-BY ZEN

The aim here is to make sense of the words shouted out of a car as their occupants speed past. *Hobatroutluv?!* Or *Gitfahrrgyapooftah!* By focussing on these mantras for a long time, repeating them over and over to yourself until you come to understand their true meaning, it is possible after a while to achieve higher Aussie Zen consciousness.

THE WORLD
we live in
is but the world
that lives in us.

DAISY BATES

THE SCRUM
Zen Meditation 2

Like Zen, the art of the scrum aims at simplification. It consists of twelve men, in ying and yang uniforms, adopting the searching position. The meditation itself is practiced on a simple grass field called "the paddock" by the big boys – taking them out of the game for a few seconds.

To the outside world the scrum is viewed as an aggressive act, but to the inner world it is a total clearing of the mind of all excess thought and feeling. It only lasts a few moments. There is an intent to get to that higher level, when the two sides of the scrum grab each other in a desire to elevate themselves onto the astral plane.

"The scrum," writes Henry Everingham, "is a ritual never performed privately. It is invariably performed in a very public situation; the sole desire being a need to reach enlightenment. And like true

zealots this is their final goal. The quickest and most effective way to attain Nirvana is by collectively smashing their heads together."

I HAVE HUMPED
my bluey in all the States
With my old black billy, the best of mates.
On roads that are rough and hilly,
With my plain and sensible,
Indispensable
Old black billy.

E.P. HARRINGTON

DAMPER

The essence of Zen simplicity

Bush bread or damper is cooked in the dying ashes of a fire.

>8 cups SR flour
>
>4 teaspoons salt
>
>2 tablespoon sugar
>
>1^1/$_2$ cup milk
>
>1^1/$_2$ cup water

Mix dry ingredients together, make a well in the centre and pour in milk and water. Using a knife, mix the dough and knead into a round shape. Place in greased camp oven dish. Cut a deep cross on the top. Cover with lid and bake in campfire ashes until ready.

Accompany with scalding hot mugs of billy tea.

ENLIGHTENMENT

Australian Zen is filled with examples of unexpected things that trigger enlightenment – it could be standing in a pub without knowing how you actually got there, picking up a girl at a party without having said a word all night, or driving around some country road without concern about the fact that you're totally lost. One of the best descriptions of the actual experience of enlightenment comes from Australian Zen Master Jerzy Skrzynsky: "One day I wiped out all European notions from my mind. I gave up my Alfa. I discarded all the ties which I thought matched my suits. I felt a little uneasy – as if I were climbing a mountain in thongs – and then, bang! It happened. I could feel myself turning into an Australian. I spoke, but my words had a broad, dry kind of feeling. I saw a variety of people coming towards me, but no one appeared to be badly dressed any more. Everyone seemed okay! I had never known such a state. And then, suddenly, I found myself repeating a wonderful mantra: No worries, no

worries, no worries, worries, no worries, no worries, no worries, no worries, no worries, no worries, no worries, no worries, no worries, no worries, no worries, no worries, no worries, no worries, no worries, no worries, no worries, no worries, no worries, worries, no worries, no worries, no worries, no worries, no worries, no worries, no worries, no worries, no worries, no worries, no worries, no worries, no worries, no worries, no worries, no worries, worries, no worries, no worries, no worries, no worries, no worries, no worries, no worries, no worries, no worries, no worries, no worries, no worries, no worries, no worries, no worries, no worries, worries, no worries, no worries, no worries, no worries, no worries, no worries, no worries, no worries, no worries, no worries, no worries, no worries, no worries."

ALMOST ZEN

A corked hat with some blow flies
around it.

EDUCATION,

to be of any value,
must be useless in the first place.

NETTIE PALMER

AUSSIE ZEN
Vocabulary 1

OZ: Cosmic earth, terrestrial earth; the spot where Vegemite comes from; a central concept of Australian Zen.

GODZONE: The Country; the source of wealth; the ultimate place.

DOWN UNDER: A mythical place occupying exactly the same space as Australia but living in a parallel universe to it and filled with backpackers and tourists. Not to be confused with Oz.

BLUE: A dialogue between Australian Zen Masters trying to find the solution to an existential problem.

HOWZAT!: Collected mass concentration in which subject is no different from object. A question with an exclamation mark.

RIPPER: seal of enlightenment; an Australian Zen Master's official confirmation that a student or a thing has reached Aussie Zen consciousness.

BLUDGING: Refers to a person's endeavor to attain enlightenment through someone else's efforts.

DUNNY: An Australian Zen study hall.

WHEN A BALL

comes at you at 120 miles an hour,
you have no time to think.
It's what makes cricket Zen.

BRIAN PERRETT

REALITY

is for people who can't handle cricket.

COUNTRY ZEN

We plough, and sow, and harrow –
Then sit down and pray for rain:
And then we all get flooded out
And have to start again.

TOM SPENCER

MEDDLE NOT
in the affairs of bunyips
for you are crunchy
and good with ketchup.

MYTHIC ZEN

THE ZEN OF VEGEMITE
Meditation 2

That which looks Zen may not be Zen; that which does
not appear Zen is Zen. Such is the case of Vegemite.
Its nine ingredients are capable of expressing metaphysical feelings and sudden flashes of Australian
Zen. There is no symbolism in Vegemite. There is no
egotism either; Vegemite is practically foodless. What
is fascinating about Vegemite is that no matter how you
spread it, it is still Vegemite. It catches life as it
spreads. And spreads. Paper thin, a centimetre thick
or in dollops it is still Vegemite. It has a universal
quality: it can be spread on white bread, brown bread,
toast, focaccia, pita, bagels, sesame rolls and on black
boots.

39

VERY ZEN

Contemplating blowflies.

THE EIGHT-FOLD PATH

The noble eight-fold righteous path:
right of way, right as rain, too right, dead right, about
right, sitting right, bang to rights and she'll be right.

FEM ZEN

You are only liberated
when you realize
just how awful you are.

GERMAINE GREER

CREATION
Australian Zen Parable

A famous geologist gave a lecture on what lay deep underneath Australia. He explained to his audience how the earth consists of concentric shells surrounding a central core divided into two parts, an inner and an outer core which is liquid, with Australia itself sitting atop the outer crust on a tectonic plate.

"Rubbish!" interrupted Auntie Jacky from the audience.

"And why is it rubbish?" inquired the geologist.

"Because everyone knows that Australia is not sitting on a tectonic plate but on a giant wombat."

"Really!" smiled superciliously the geologist. "And if that is so what is the giant wombat standing on?"

"On an even bigger wombat."

"And that wombat?" smirked the geologist.

"On a humungous wombat."

"I see!" exclaimed the famous geologist, winking at the audience and thinking that now he'd stumped

43

the little old person at the back of the hall. "And how exactly is the humungous wombat resting on the earth's core then?"

"Don't you understand anything, mate?" replied Auntie Jacky. "It's wombats all the way!"

FROM: THE WOMBAT AND THE CREATION OF THE UNIVERSE

OH,

who would be a pudding,
A pudding in a pot,
A pudding which is stood on
A fire which is hot?
Oh sad indeed the lot
Of puddings in a pot.

NORMAN LINDSAY

MASTER AND DISCIPLE
A Zen Conversation

"I have so many things to think about."
"What things?"
"I haven't thought about them yet but I am sure there are lots."

TASSIE ZEN

She's
apples She's
apples She's apples She's
apples She's apples She's apples She's apples
She's apples She's apples She's apples She's apples
She's apples She's apples She's apples She's apples She's
apples She's apples She's apples She's apples She's apples
She's apples She's apples She's apples She's apples She's
apples She's apples She's apples She's apples She's apples
She's apples She's apples She's apples She's apples She's
apples She's apples She's apples She's apples She's apples
She's apples She's apples She's apples She's apples She's
apples She's apples She's apples She's apples She's apples
She's apples She's apples She's apples She's apples
She's apples She's apples She's apples She's apples
She's apples She's apples She's apples She's
apples She's apples She's apples She's
apples She's apples She's apples
She's apples She's apples

ULTIMATE ZEN

When eating Vegemite,
you know you've reached Zenhood
when you cannot taste the salt.

STILLNESS

Australian Zen and the Art of Slouching

Since the time of the First Fleet, beer and Australian Zen have been connected. Fittingly, it was one of the earliest free settlers, John Boston, who brewed the first beer in 1796. And it was in 1803, the same year that Matthew Flinders suggested adopting the name Australia (meaning Southland) that the first brewery was established at Parramatta.

Like Australian Zen, the art of slouching aims at artlessness. It consists simply of leaning against a bar, ordering a beer and downing it. Economy of movement is paramount. Contrary to popular belief, Australians don't drink to get drunk. They just drink. Getting as much beer into you with as little effort as possible is essential. Don't sip. Gulp. Re-ordering must be an imperceptible nod to the barmaid.

The anchor points of the slouch are the ankle and the elbow. You've got one foot draped over the other, you've got both arms bent. You only need movement

in the elbow and the wrist. It's all about focus. What the ritual of the slouch does is turn it into a timeless exercise. It defies time. Time is abandoned. In the true Australian Zen slouch, time stands still. The only free movement you need is in the neck so that the barmaid will know that you need another drink.

WEB ZEN

The only sure sign
that there is intelligent life out there
is that they haven't tried to contact us.

VERY VERY ZEN

Stoicism in the face of personal setbacks,
but total grief at the loss of one's
favourite sports team.

SUNBAKING
Zen Meditation 3

At the heart of Australian Zen practice is lying on the beach, or "baking in oil." Though rooted in ancient meditative practices, Australian sunbaking differs from other forms of meditation in that it uses no meditation object or abstract concept for the sunbaker to focus on. The aim of sun baking is to empty the mind – the sun bather's everyday functioning mind – and then, through years of practice, to reach a state of pure, thought-free existence so that the mind can realize its own Australian Zen-nature. And unlike other forms of meditation, sunbaking is not simply a means to an end. Sunbaking "turns into gold the matter of my arm," said the poet Andrew Taylor. It transforms the body into a golden colour and, as one progresses, layer by layer the skin is removed.

CRICKETERS

it would seem are so intent on being cricketers
that they have no time to speculate on their
not being cricketers.

WILLIAM A. RUSSEL

TAB ZEN

A man walked into his local TAB. He had a couple of good tips from his wife's cousin whose best friend was the trainer of several champion horses. After a few bets he left and found that his son had grown up and got married, his daughter was finishing university and his wife was running a business.

STEPHEN CUMINES

TRUST

in your own reflection.
You'll die alone in the end, so live alone
And be a man on earth among your enemies.

DOUGLAS STEWART

THE WANDER-LIGHT

An eccentric genius revered as much for his wit as for his understanding, Henry Lawson (1867-1922) is a beloved figure. A brilliant child, he went deaf by the age of fourteen. Without any schooling, he began to write about the strange, unsettled Zen of his day:

For my ways are strange ways and new ways and old ways,
  And deep ways and steep ways and high ways and low;
    I'm at home and at ease on a track that I know not,
      And restless and lost on a road that I know.

AUSTRALIANS
are not what they seem.
Nor are they otherwise.

AUSSIE ZEN
Vocabulary 2

CLAYTONS: A mysterious substance, symbolic of the artificial and illusory nature of the world.

DINKUM: Refers to intuitive Australian Zenhood, a reflection on the inborn attainment of enlightenment.

YAKKA: Emptiness or void, without meaning, a key problem in Australian Zenhood.

MOTZA: Basic matter, the primal dough from which the world has been fashioned, a key notion of Australian Zen.

BARBIE: Collective concentration in which subject is no different from object.

RUBBIDY: A meditation hall.

MATESHIP ZEN

My wife ran off with my best friend,
I really miss him.

XMAS ZEN

I was vegetarian for about ten years. I went home to my grandmother's country house for Christmas. My grandmother was very upset that I would not eat the turkey which she had spent days preparing. In the end, I felt more compassion for my grandmother than for the turkey, and I ate the turkey.

RIDGIE-DIDGE

Australian Zen mantra used to cover
a succession of untruths.

A ZEN YARN

A man driving along a country road saw of a cyclone approaching. He jumped out of the car and took refuge under a bridge. Terrifying winds roared all around him as he hung onto the pylons. When the cyclone abated for a while he ran for the hills where his home was. Suddenly he smelt burning and realised that he was in the middle of a bushfire. He knew of a creek nearby and ran for it. He dived into the water just as all around him the bush went up in flames like a torch. Coming up only for air he crouched in the water until the bushfire roared past him. But at the very moment he tried to step ashore, a torrential flood burst down the creek bed like a deluge, sweeping everything in its wake. Bobbing helplessly in the current, just about pulled under by the horrific rip, he managed to spy a spot of high ground with something sticking out of it. He grabbed this slenderest of chances at survival but it turned out to be merely a bottle of beer wedged

between the rocks. Grasping the bottle with a desperate hand, the man pulled open the top with his teeth. "Must be my lucky day," he said. "My favourite brand."

ZEN SCHOOL

"How about another pony? I'm in the chair."
"Why not? You can't walk on one leg."

EVERYTHING

I know about Australia
I learned from eating a Vegemite sandwich.

JOHN IRONBARK

WRAP ME UP

in my stockwhip and blanket
And bury me deep down below
Where the farm implement salesmen won't molest me,
In the shades where the cooler bars grow.

LENNIE LOWER

CUTE ZEN

Attractiveness is a quality that is difficult to analyze and impossible to define, but the Koala has it. It is like a bear, yet nothing like a bear. Its stocky built, like a fat baby, and its coat of dense yet fluffy fur make it look cuddlesome; its naked black nose, like the leather toe-cap of a well polished old shoe, and the little twinkling eyes several sizes too small for our normal conception of an animal make it look like a made-up toy, and the complete absence of a tail just adds to its quaintness.

PHIL MORRISON

VEGIE ZEN

Life is like a cabbage –
you can peel away its outer layers
but you will never find its deeper meaning.

THE ONE THING

that helps me keep my slender grip
on reality is the close friendship I share with my
collection of singing potatoes.

WEB ZEN

THE TEN PRECEPTS

The ten noble precepts: not to cadge, not to dob, not to big note yourself, not to bung it on, not to put the bite on, not to cause problems, not to whinge, not to crawl, not to have tickets on yourself, not to buzz around like a blue-arsed fly.

NO PROBLEMS

The second most popular mantra in Australian Zen. Can be an answer to a request, it can be a response to a situation, but most often No Problem is an answer to a question that has not been asked. That is the Zen of it.

THE MORE
you own,
the less you understand.

DAVID JONES

BUSH ZEN

Toujours, toujours gum tree!

SIR ED THOMSON

A DIAMOND
is beautiful and made to last forever,
but you can't cook on it.

FOLK ZEN

URBAN ZEN

"The dinkum Aussie judges a man by what he does, not by who he is," said the man from the bush.

"The real dinkum Aussie does not judge," replied his mate from the city.

ACCEPTANCE

Two family men who rejected the comforts of city life and sought a land route across the mysterious heart of the continent that no white man had ever traversed, Robert O'Hara Burke (1821-1861) and William John Wills (1834-1861) would inspire countless others. One bright day, the two men left Melbourne with a large party of men to begin a long journey across Australia all the way to the Gulf of Carpentaria. All except John King perished on the return trip at Cooper Creek.

Wills seems to have known that he would not leave the desert alive and wrote a matter-of-fact letter to his father from Cooper Creek where he was slowly dying of hunger and thirst. "These are probably the last lines you will ever get from me. We are on the point of starvation, not so much from absolute want of food, but for want of nutriment in what we can get." And having signed his name, he added the following note:

"I think to live about four or five days. My religious views are not the least changed and I have not the least fear of their being so. My spirits are excellent."

Burke and Wills spent their last five days living under the fiery sun of the desert. On the final day Burke announced that it was time to die and got himself fully prepared, asking the sole surviving member of the expedition to remain with him until the end. "It is my wish," he said, "that you should place the pistol in my right hand, and that you leave me unburied as I lie."

I COME
from the Northern plains
Where the girls and grass are scanty;
Where the creeks run dry or ten foot high
And it's either drought or plenty.

BUSH SONG

BALMAIN ZEN

As you know, Balmain boys don't cry.

NEVILLE WRAN

REALITY

Just as in Buddhist Zen there is no outside reality, in Australian Zen there is no reality outside of Australia. And just as in Eastern Zen you are told that being happy or sad or worried or miserable or depressed is an illusion, the same thing is true for Australia, where you only think you're travelling to London or New York or Shanghai or Paris or Bali, but it's just an illusion. The only reality is here in Australia.

DIGNITY

A crawler's a crawler everywhere,
but a man is a man even in jail.

HENRY LAWSON

IT IS ONLY
in sport that many Australians express
those approaches to life that are un-Australian
if expressed in any other connection.

DONALD HORNE

"COME TELL ME NOW,
what is Christmas Day?"
"It's the day before the races out at Tangmalangaloo."

JOHN O'BRIEN

SOUL ZEN

Thapolo.
Wari wanjinju.
Allinger yerra-bamalla.
Illa booker mer ley urrie urrie.

WE JUST

have to stumble on blindly with God's mercy
raining down on us like thunderbolts.

PETER KENNA

AUSSIE ZEN
Vocabulary 3

PIECE OF CAKE: Intuitive wisdom, insight into the future or the true outcome of events; a key notion of Australian Tradesman Zen.

NO WORRIES: The Australian Zen utterance for 'Yes'.

GALAH: No mind, or detachment of mind, complete freedom from focussed thinking.

LAID BACK: An advanced being who can't even be bothered with Nirvana.

PLONKO: A being whose only concern is getting into Nirvana.

NIRVANA: Bottle-shop on Bondi Beach.

BUCKLEY'S: Literally "Buckley's Chance," the Australian Zen term for the pessimistic philosophy of Arthur Schopenhauer.

RAFFERTY'S RULES: The Existential Chaos philosophy of Sartre, Camus and Rafferty.

ALTHOUGH

most Australians have not even seen their deserts,
the stoicism of the desert seems to have
entered their souls.

DONALD HORNE

PLAYING SPORTS

The highest form of patriotism in Australia.

JOHN IRONBARK

EVERYONE'S
entitled to life
liberty
and the pursuit of horse-racing.

BANJO PATTERSON

Australian Zen

Kookaburra sits in the old gum tree,
Merry merry queen of the bush is she,
Laugh, kookaburra, laugh, kookaburra,
Gay your life must be.

MARION SINCLAIR

BLOKEY ZEN

Those who aspire to attain Australian Zenhood at the earliest possible opportunity may contemplate on the exhortation given to the Sentimental Bloke:

> Livin' an' lovin'; learnin' to fergive
> The deeds an' words of some un'appy bloke
> Who's missed the bus—so 'ave I come to live,
> An' take the 'ole mad world as 'arf a joke.

C.J. DENNIS

NOBODY

wants to die while there's rum in the bottle.

DOUGLAS STEWART

WINE AND BEER
are different only
if you haven't drunk enough.

JOHN IRONBARK

BEER

makes you feel
as you ought to feel without beer.

HENRY LAWSON

YOU CAN

lead a horse to drink,
but you can't make it water.

JOH BJELKE-PETERSEN

IT'S LATE

and too late to be crying for what we've done;
it's what we'll do next that matters.

DOUGLAS STEWART

A ZEN HERO

Ned Kelly (1855-1880) is one of the most beloved figures in Australian folk tradition. He loved the bush, his mother and robbing banks, which he called "the highest form of Zen".

After receiving the seal of enlightenment from his jail warden, Ned chose not to lead a civilian life but to emulate the bushrangers of old, living in discomfort as an outlaw and relying on robbery as a sustenance. He endured bitter periods of harassment, yet he never lost his extraordinary fatalism and sense of Australian Zenhood. When a judge sentenced him to hanging, after he was found guilty, Ned intoned the greatest Aussie Zen haiku:

> It is not that I fear death;
> I fear it as little
> As to drink a cup of tea.

Ned also left behind his "Great Aussie Essence", as in the celebrated story about his final moments. As he was led to the gallows, everyone expected Ned to show a reaction, but his face remained immobile. It was only when the hangman placed the noose around his neck that Ned looked the assembled audience in the eyes. "Such," he taught them, "is life!"

PARADISE
is exactly like Australia,
only more crowded.

BEING

at last on our way,
A great calmness came upon my soul,
As if all creation waited on my will.
I was at that moment made whole.

WILLIAM HART-SMITH

BACKPACKER ZEN

A number of years ago a backpacker was making his way through the country. He claimed to be a gold miner on his way from Ballarat to Kalgoorlie in Western Australia.

In Bendigo he asked at the Cricketer's Arms, "How far is it to Kalgoorlie?" He was told, "It's three months on foot, mate, but if you cut through the Wagga shopping centre, you'll save a quarter of an hour."

So in order to save the quarter of an hour he went by way of Wagga. Not such a bad idea, when you think of it. If you don't take advantage of the little benefits of life, you'll never get any big ones.

And then, as the saying goes, a backpacker can never take a wrong turn.

YOB ZEN

One time a mate asked Paddy Hannan to show him the kind of Zen he practiced in his archery. Paddy took up his bow and took aim at the target. As he was about to shoot, he unexpectedly turned ninety degrees, aimed at his best friend and started laughing. With the spiked deadly arrow pointing straight at him, the friend began to quake in fear. But then, in an inspiration of his own Zen consciousness, and borrowing a leaf from William Tell, he balanced his beer on the top of his head setting Paddy a new target. And at that moment he became enlightened into Yob Zen.

ONE

man's fate today, may be another's tomorrow.
We are all in it up to the neck together,
and we know it.

FREDERIC MANNING

THE BEST WAY

to tell gold is to pass the nugget around
a crowded bar, and ask them if it's gold.
If it comes back, it's not gold.

LENNIE LOWER

AUSSIE ZEN
Vocabulary 4

JONAH: The Australian Zen universal law of cause and effect.

RILEY: One of the few deities of Australian Zen thinking; the life of Riley; imitating Riley is akin to imitating the Buddha. A central concept.

THE BUSH: The source of Australian Zen; freedom from yakka; extinction of all repayments; the realization of the true nature of motza.

LARRY: The One; happy as Larry; the god of joy; the ultimate principle.

BONDI BEACH: The Way; the origins of reality; the truth; the ultimate place of pilgrimage.

I EAT

my peas with honey
I've done so all my life
It makes the peas taste funny
But it keeps them on the knife.

FOLK ZEN

HIGH SOCIETY ZEN

When the guest of honor is a man, he should take the hostess's arm when entering the dining room. If the hostess is very far gone, another gentleman may hold the other arm, a third gentleman going in front with the legs. The trick is to find three gentlemen in one room.

LENNIE LOWER

SENTIMENTAL ZEN

I've studied books wiv yearnings to improve,
  To 'eave meself out of me lowly groove,
  An' 'ere is orl the change I ever got:
" 'Ark at yer 'eart, an' you kin learn the lot."

C.J. DENNIS

FroZen

David Edgeworth and Douglas Mawson were members of Shackleton's first Antarctic expedition. En route to locating the Magnetic South Pole, they struck tent among the ice mountains of the region. While Mawson was in his tent, he heard Edgeworth calling quietly from somewhere outside.

"Mawson!"

Mawson, who was re-loading his camera, ignored however the call. A few minutes later he heard again:

"Mawson!"

Once again he ignored it. Finally, he heard Edgeworth's voice faintly from somewhere far away:

"Well, Mawson, I am in a rather dangerous position, I am really hanging on by my fingers to the edge of a crevasse, and I don't think I can hold on much longer, I shall have to trouble you to assist me."

One can imagine Mawson calling back: "Hang on, I won't be a tick!" and Edgeworth awaiting rescue without an additional word of complaint, knowing that an Australian tick can be as long as an hour.

And that is the Zen of it.

NEVER ADMIT
the pain,
Bury it deep;
Only the weak complain,
Complaint is cheap.

MARY GILMORE

NATURE

The dominant note of Australian scenery is
weird melancholy.

MARCUS CLARKE

OUTBACK ZEN

There are mirages back of Bourke so real that when the camels rush for them, the poor brutes bounce back off them and return with big bruises on their foreheads. There are places out West so hot that thermometers have to be kept in the ice chests so they won't burst. There are places where they whip the cream with stockwhips and men ride 1800 miles for a permanent wave.

LENNIE LOWER

LIFE'S

wot yeh make it; an' the bloke 'oo tries
To grab the shinin' stars frum out the skies
Goes crook on life, an' calls the world a cheat,
An' tramples on the daisies at 'is feet.

C.J. DENNIS

When you can't laugh, you're dead.

BEATRICE FAUST

POLITICAL ZEN

Rookwood cemetery is full of indispensable men.

BEN CHIFLEY

TRUE ZEN

I fought for nothing and I won.

HARRY HOOTON

REQUIEM

I have left out the wattle – because it wasn't there. I have also neglected to mention the heart-broken old mate, with his grizzled head bowed and great pearly drops streaming down his rugged cheeks. He was absent – he was probably outback. For similar reasons I have omitted reference to the suspicious moisture in the eyes of a bearded bush ruffian named Bill. Bill failed to turn up, and the only moisture was that which was induced by the heat. I have left out the "sad Australian sunset" because the sun was not going down at the time. The burial took place exactly at midday.

HENRY LAWSON

THERE IS NO END

where there is a beginning.
Beginning must follow end.
Endlessly.

PATRICK WHITE

SOURCES

For further readings into the works of the authors quoted

❧ p.8 *Here's Another* by Lennie Lower (1903-1947) ❧ p.12 *It is great to be alive* by Harry Hooton (1908-1961) ❧ p.13 *A Metaphysical Song* by Adam Lindsay Gordon (1833-1870) ❧ p.16 *Sydney Morning Herald* 13 July 1903 ❧ p.19 *The Call of the City* by Victor Daley (1858-1905) ❧ p.20 *Five Days Old* by Francis Webb (1925-1973) ❧ p.21 *The Bachelor's Guide to the Care of the Young* by Lennie Lower ❧ p.22 *Australia* by Sir Keith Hancock ❧ p.24 *Daisy Bates* by Elizabeth Salter ❧ p.27 *My Old Black Billy* by Edward Phillip Harrington (1896-1966) ❧ p.32 *Taking it Over* by Janet Gertrude Palmer (1885-1964) ❧ p.35 *Café Tropicana* June 1999 ❧ p.37 *How M'Dougal Topped the Score* by Thomas Edward Spencer (1845-1911) ❧ p.42 *The Australian* 15 September 1985 ❧ p.45 *The Magic Pudding* by Norman Lindsay (1879-1869) ❧ p.54 *The Bulletin* March 1991 ❧ p.56 *Ned Kelly* by Douglas Stewart (1913-1985) ❧ p.57 *The Wander-Light* by Henry Lawson (1867-1922) ❧ p.66 *Trade Union Annual* 1961 by John Ironbark (Russ Singleton) (?-?) ❧ p.67 *Where the Cooler Bars Grow* by Lennie Lower ❧ p.68 *Along the Track* by Philip Morrison (1900-1958) ❧ p.74 *Our Antipodes* by Sir Edward Thomson (1800-1879) ❧ p.80 *Sydney Morning Herald* 13 June 1983 ❧ p.82 *One-hundred-and-three* by Henry Lawson ❧ p.83 *Southern Exposure* by Donald Horne (1921-) ❧ p.84 *Tangmalangaloo* by John O'Brien (the Very Reverend Joseph Hartigan) (1879-1952) ❧ p.85 *Soul Zen*, Anonymous ❧ p.86 *A Hard God* by Peter Kenna (1930-1993) ❧ p.89 *Southern Exposure* by Donald Horne ❧ p.90 *The Unionist* June 1962 ❧ p.91 *The Bulletin* August 1899 ❧ p.92 *World Jamboree Magazine* 1934 quoting Marion Sinclair (1896-1988) ❧ p.93 *The Sentimental Bloke* by C.J. Dennis (1876-1938) ❧ p.94 *Ned Kelly* by Douglas Stewart ❧ p.95 *P.K.I. Annual* 1964 ❧ p.97 *The Little Book of Aussie Wisdom* quoting Johannes Bjelke-

Petersen (1911-) ❦ p.98 *Ned Kelly* by Douglas Stewart ❦ p.102 *Departure* by William Hart-Smith (1911-1990) ❦ p.105 *The Middle Parts of Fortune...* by Frederic Manning (1882-1935) ❦ p.106 *What Gold Is* by Lennie Lower ❦ p.109 *Guide to Etiquette* by Lennie Lower ❦ p.109 *The Sentimental Bloke* by C.J. Dennis ❦ p.113 *Never Admit the Pain* by Dame Mary Gilmore (1865-1962) ❦ p.114 *Preface to Adam Lindsay Gordon's Verses* by Marcus Clarke (Andrew Hislop) (1846-1881) ❦ p.115 *Out Dubbo Way* by Lennie Lower ❦ p.116 *The Sentimental Bloke* by C.J. Dennis ❦ p.117 from *The Little Book of Aussie Wisdom* quoting Beatrice Faust (1939-) ❦ p.118 *Inside Canberra* 1983 quoting Ben Chifley ❦ p.119 *The Promised Land* by Harry Hooton ❦ p.120 *The Union Buries its Dead* by Henry Lawson ❦ p.121 *The Ham Funeral* by Patrick White (1912-1990) ❦

ALSO IN THIS SERIES

HOW TO SURVIVE AUSTRALIA

A guide for the newcomer, the old timer and the bewildered in betweens

As every experienced traveller knows, Australia is a safe continent of gentle marsupials, beautiful sites and freedom-loving inhabitants. Few travellers will realize, however, just what a responsibility they are taking on by not knowing the do's and don'ts of society. So Robert Treborlang has kindly provided them with this invaluable handbook full of advice on how not to ask questions, how not to dress well, how to act busy or make a cup of tea.

The book emphasizes the importance of being low key – not to mention rules for behaving at parties and dinner invitations – for a thoughtless person could easily upset the sensitivities of the shy and amiable locals. Here is a funny collection of helpful hints and rules to give everyone a new insight into life on the world's oldest, smallest and most unusual continent.

ISBN 1 875614 10 9

ALSO IN THIS SERIES

ONLY IN AUSTRALIA

*At last, the book to tell you
everything you always suspected was
different about Australia*

Singleness has been Australia's hallmark from
its inception – and continues to this day!
"Only In Australia" gives an amusing picture
of the uniqueness of our times, past and
present. Read about: The strange events that
led to the creation of the Sydney Opera House,
why Vegemite was used on boils, why koalas
pine to death for the love of a mate, how
Snowtown got its name, and where the world's
Royals come to hide.

"Only In Australia" offers many new and
hitherto hidden facts. And in an astounding
age of information, the author Robert Treborlang holds up an engaging mirror for one and
all and shows how the smallest continent can
be at the same time great in surprises and
unique in the facts that shaped its destiny.

ISBN 1 875614 20 6